Science Alive!
air

CRABTREE
Publishing Company
www.crabtreebooks.com

How to use this book

Each chapter begins with experiments, followed by the explanation of the scientific concepts used in the experiments. Each experiment is graded according to its difficulty level. A level 4 or 5 means adult assistance is advised. Difficult words are in boldface and explained in the glossary on page 32.

Crabtree Publishing
www.crabtreebooks.com

PMB 16A, 350 Fifth Avenue,
Suite 3308, New York
New York 10118

612 Welland Avenue,
St. Catharines, Ontario
Canada L2M 5V6

**Published in 2003
by Crabtree Publishing Company**

Published with Times Editions
Copyright © 2003 by Times Media Private Limited

Series originated and designed by
TIMES EDITIONS
An imprint of Times Media Private Limited
A member of the Times Publishing Group

Coordinating Editor: Ellen Rodger
Project Editors: P. A. Finlay, Carrie Gleason
Production Coordinator: Rosie Gowsell
Series Writers: Darlene Lauw, Lim Cheng Puay
Series Editor: Oh Hwee Yen
Title Editor: Oh Hwee Yen
Series Designer: Rosie Francis
Series Picture Researcher: Susan Jane Manuel

Cataloging-in-Publication Data
Lauw, Darlene.
    Air / Darlene Lauw and Lim Cheng Puay.
        p. cm. — (Science alive!)
    Summary: Uses simple experiments to demonstrate the properties of air including air pressure and expansion, how flight is achieved, and how rust is produced.
    Includes bibliographical references and index.
    ISBN 0-7787-0566-8 (RLB) — ISBN 0-7787-0612-5 (PB)
    1. Air—Juvenile literature. [1. Air—Experiments. 2. Experiments.] I. Lim, Cheng Puay.
II. Title.
QC161.2 .L38 2003
533'.6—dc21

2002011580
LC

Picture Credits
Marc Crabtree: cover; Art Directors & Trip Photo Library: 7 (middle), 23 (middle), 26–27, 30 (top); Bes Stock: 6–7, 10–11, 11, 15 (middle); David Simson: 30–31; Hulton Archive: 15 (top); Photobank Photolibrary/Singapore: 1, 14, 18–19, 19, 22–23; Science Photo Library: 27 (top)

Printed and bound in Malaysia
1 2 3 4 5 6—0S—07 06 05 04 03 02

INTRODUCTION

Air is all around us. Air is a mixture of several invisible gases including nitrogen, oxygen, and carbon dioxide. We cannot see, smell, or taste air, but we can see and feel the effects of it. Air changes the way objects look, feel, and move. How does air make rust? Does air have weight? How does air help airplanes and kites fly? Find out the answers to all these questions by doing the fun activities in this book!

Contents

What is air?

Air is a mixture of invisible gases including oxygen, carbon dioxide, and nitrogen. We take about eighteen breaths of air in one minute. When we inhale, or breathe air in, we fill our lungs with all the gases in the air. Oxygen, nitrogen, and carbon dioxide remain inside our bodies when we exhale, or breathe air out. The most important of these gases is oxygen. We need oxygen to survive. Fire also needs oxygen for it to burn. Ask an adult to help you with this experiment!

Flame on, flame out!

■ Ask an adult for help

Difficult – 5
– 4
Moderate – 3
– 2
Easy – 1

You will need:
- A lighter or matches
- A candle
- A candle holder
- A glass jar

1 Ask an adult to light the candle on the candle holder. Let the flame burn for a couple of minutes. Place the open mouth of the jar over the flame. What do you see?

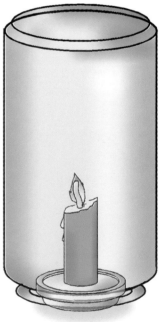

2 Just before the flame goes out completely, ask an adult to help you lift the jar away. Now, what do you see?

How do iron nails rust? Find out how air helps make rust!

■ Ask an adult for help

Difficult – 5
– 4
Moderate – 3
– 2
Easy – 1

You will need:
- Two glass jars with lids
- Tap water
- Six iron nails
- A cooking pot
- A stove or hotplate
- Oven mitts
- Cooking oil

Rusting nails

 Fill one jar with tap water. Place three nails in the water. Screw the lid on the jar.

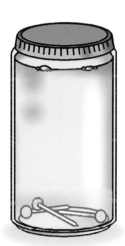

2 Fill the other jar with tap water, and put the other three nails in the jar. Fill half the pot with water. Place the second jar without the lid in the pot, and heat the pot on the stove.

3 When the water in the jar starts to boil, ask an adult to remove the jar from the pot using the oven mitts.

4 Pour a small amount of cooking oil in the jar of boiled water, so that it forms a thin layer on the water surface. Screw the lid on the jar.

5 Leave the two jars to stand for about two weeks. What do you see after this time?

5

The need for oxygen

Some **chemical reactions**, such as burning and rusting, need oxygen. In the experiment *Flame On, Flame Out*, the oxygen supply was cut off when you placed the jar over the candle. Did you notice that the flame started to go out? The oxygen that was left in the jar was being used up as the candle burned. When you lifted the jar, the flame lit up again, because oxygen rushed to the flame.

The combination of iron and oxygen produces rust. This process is called **oxidation**. Objects in water are exposed to oxygen because water is made up of hydrogen and oxygen **molecules**. In the experiment *Rusting Nails*, boiling the water in the second jar removed most of the oxygen in the water. When you added oil to the jar, the oil floated on the surface of the water, preventing air from entering the water. Only the nails in the first jar rusted because there was oxygen in the water.

Most plants cannot use the nitrogen in the air because it is tightly bound to other gas molecules, such as those of oxygen. Farmers often add nitrogen-rich fertilizer to soil to grow crops.

Other gases in air

The air around us is made up mainly of two gases: nitrogen and oxygen. As well as these two gases, there are small amounts of eight other gases in air, including **water vapor** and carbon dioxide.

Nitrogen and carbon dioxide are necessary for plants to survive. Plants need carbon dioxide to make food, and nitrogen is one of the main nutrients plants need to grow. Some plants, including peas and beans, have **bacteria** that convert the nitrogen in the air into a form that plants can use.

QUIZTIME

Paul bought a model train with many iron and steel parts. What can he do to prevent it from rusting?

Answer: He can paint the model! One way of preventing rust from occurring is to prevent steel or iron from coming in contact with oxygen. Adding a barrier, such as paint, between the iron, steel, and air is one way to prevent rusting.

Did you know?

Some of the other gases in air are not needed for survival, but are useful to us in other ways. The gases helium, neon, argon, xenon, and krypton help make **fluorescent** lights and neon signs. When electricity, a form of energy, flows through a tube containing these gases, the gases glow and produce a colorful light. Different gases give off different colored light. Neon gases produce red light. Argon gas glows in shades of green, yellow, and white.

Any object that is exposed to air is exposed to the oxygen in air. This is why iron nails rust (*above*) when they are left in the open for a long time.

RED, RUSTY ROCKS

Iron occurs naturally in rocks. Small pieces of iron react with oxygen in the air to form rust, giving the rocks a reddish color. Did you know that the red color on the surface of Mars comes from rock rust? Oxidation uses up so much of the oxygen on Mars that there is almost no oxygen surrounding the planet!

How much oxygen in air?

Y ou know that air is made up of nitrogen, oxygen, and small amounts of other gases. The other gases make up less than one percent of air, and nitrogen makes up 78 percent. What percent of oxygen is there in air? Find out how steel wool helps us measure the amount of oxygen in air.

Rusty steel wool

Difficult – 5
– 4
Moderate – 3
– 2
Easy – 1

You will need:
- Duct tape
- A strip of wire mesh, measuring 0.4 X 8 inches (1 X 20.3 cm)
- A glass
- Steel wool
- Tongs
- A bowl of vinegar
- A large bowl
- A blue marker
- A red marker

1 Tape the wire mesh around the mouth of the glass as shown in the diagram.

2 Soak the steel wool in the bowl of vinegar for one minute. Using the tongs, remove the steel wool from the vinegar. Shake the steel wool to get rid of the excess vinegar.

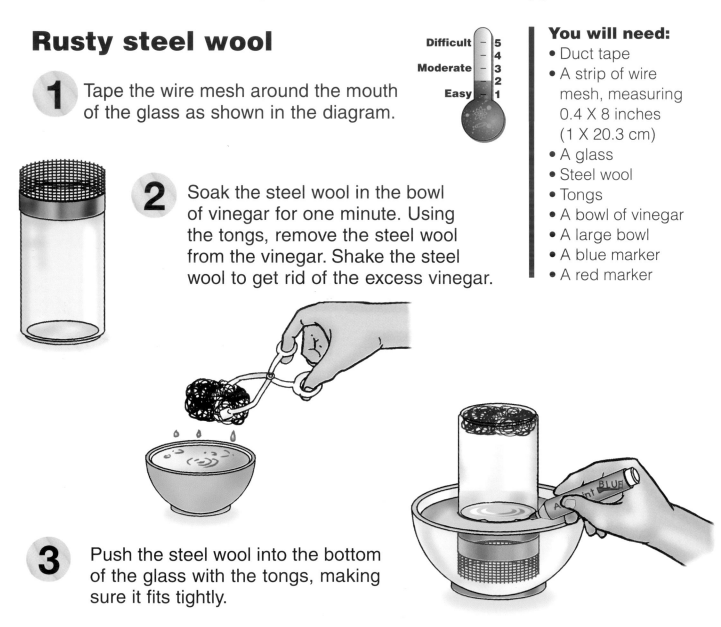

3 Push the steel wool into the bottom of the glass with the tongs, making sure it fits tightly.

4 Pour some water into the bowl, and then slowly place the glass upside down in the bowl. On the side of the glass, make a mark with the blue marker where the water level in the glass is.

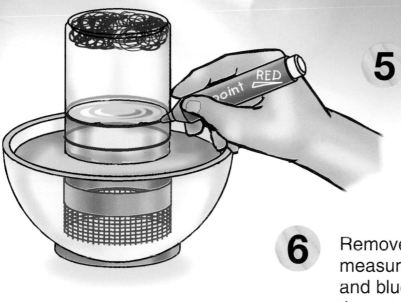

5 After a day or two, note the water level. What do you see? Has the water level changed? Mark the new water level using the red marker.

6 Remove the glass from the bowl and measure the distance between the red and blue marks. Record the difference in the notebook. This is the change in water level before and after the wool rusted

 7 Measure the distance between the blue mark and the bottom of the jar, and write your measurement in the notebook. This is the original water level.

 8 Divide the change in water level by the original water level. This is the amount of space the oxygen in the glass takes up.

$$\frac{\text{Change in water level}}{\text{Original water level}} = \text{Percentage of oxygen in the glass}$$

Measuring oxygen

Steel is a mixture of iron and a material called carbon. In the experiment *Rusty Steel Wool*, the iron in the wool combined with the oxygen in the glass to form rust. As the oxygen was used up, water in the bowl seeped into the glass and replaced the oxygen, causing the water level to rise. What number did you get when you measured the change in the water level, and divided it by the original water level? Did you find that your calculations worked out to approximately one-fifth? This is correct as oxygen makes up nearly one-fifth, or 21 percent, of air.

The percentage of oxygen in air is the same whether we are at sea level or on a mountain. As we climb higher up a mountain, there is less air, so there is less oxygen.

Where does oxygen come from?

Plants are the only living things that produce oxygen. Green plants produce most of the oxygen found in our environment. Green plants use sunlight and carbon dioxide to produce sugar, the main source of energy for plants. This process, known as **photosynthesis**, releases oxygen.

Did you know?
The air surrounding Earth is called the atmosphere. The atmosphere becomes thinner with increasing height. Mountain climbers have to breathe harder as they climb higher up a mountain in order for their lungs to inhale enough oxygen. To ensure that they get enough oxygen, mountain climbers sometimes carry oxygen tanks.

GREEN PLANTS AND GREENHOUSE GASES

Green plants help clean the air we breathe by absorbing carbon dioxide and releasing oxygen. Carbon dioxide is an odorless gas made from oxygen and carbon. It is produced when animals exhale and decay after death. Carbon dioxide also comes from vehicle exhaust and factory smoke. Carbon dioxide is a **greenhouse gas** that traps heat in Earth's atmosphere. Carbon dioxide dissolves in rain, oceans, and lakes, forming a weak acid that harms ocean and lake life.

Air changes when heated

When air is heated, it expands, or spreads out. Air also becomes lighter, or less **dense**, when it is heated, so it rises. When air cools, it contracts, or moves closer together, and becomes heavier. You can see the effects of air expansion and contraction in this experiment.

Swoosh! Into the bottle

■ Ask an adult for help

Difficult — 5
— 4
Moderate — 3
— 2
Easy — 1

You will need:
- A hard-boiled egg, peeled
- A clear glass bottle with a wide mouth
- Three matches

1 Find an egg that is slightly larger than the opening of the bottle. Ask an adult to help you light the matches and drop them into the bottle.

2 Let the matches burn. Place the egg, with its pointed end facing downward, into the mouth of the bottle.

3 Press lightly on the egg to make sure the egg totally seals the opening of the bottle. Watch what happens. The egg slips right into the bottle!

The same principle of heated air that let the egg slip into the bottle explains how a hot-air balloon stays in flight. What keeps a hot-air balloon in the sky? Air expansion!

Up, up and away!

You will need:
- A screwdriver
- A small paper cup
- Four strings, each 8 inches (20.3 cm) long
- A large thin plastic bag
- A pebble
- A friend
- A hair dryer

 1 Using the screwdriver, poke four holes in the top edge of the paper cup. Knot one string in each of the holes as shown in the diagram. Tie the four strings to the handles of the plastic bag. Put the pebble into the cup to act as a weight.

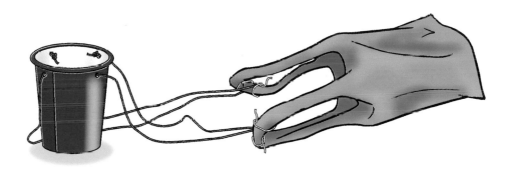

2 Ask a friend to hold the bag open while you fill it with hot air from the hair dryer. Use the hottest setting on the dryer and hold it just below the opening of the bag. Release the bag and watch it float!

Can you change the size of air?

Heat causes air molecules to move faster and farther apart, or expand. When air cools, it contracts, and the molecules move slower and closer together. In the experiment *Swoosh! Into the Bottle*, the flame from the matches caused the air to heat up and expand. Some of the hot air rose and escaped from the bottle. The remaining air in the bottle cooled and contracted, creating a pulling **force** that sucked the egg into the bottle.

Can you change the weight of air?

Hot air is lighter because it weighs less than cool air. In the experiment *Up, Up and Away*, the hot air from the hair dryer filled the bag. The bag was then full of warm air that was lighter than the cooler air surrounding the bag, so the warm air in the bag rose and carried the hot-air balloon upward.

First flight with hot air

In 1783, two French brothers, Joseph Montgolfier (1740–1810) and Jacques Étienne Montgolfier (1745–1799) invented the first hot-air balloon. They started experimenting with hot air when they saw that a shirt drying by the fire could rise into the air. The brothers' first hot-air balloon was made of a lightweight cloth. The first flight took place in September, 1783, and carried a rooster, a sheep, and a duck. The hot-air balloon flew more than 1.5 miles (2.5 km) for eight minutes, and reached a height of 6.6 feet (2 m) above the ground.

QUIZTIME

Why is a hot-air balloon flying in bright sunlight dangerous?

Answer: As the sun heats the hot air inside the balloon, it may expand to the point of bursting! Hot-air balloon makers build safety valves in the balloons to release air if the balloon expands too much.

Did you know?
Birds such as falcons (*right*) and eagles soar in the sky by riding on hot air rising from the ground! They fly into pockets of rising hot air, which carry the birds into the sky. Birds can conserve, or save, their energy if they do not have to fly against the wind. Seabirds also use wind power to help them rest in the air.

EL NIÑO, HOT AIR OVER HOT WATER

Every few years, around December, fish living along the west coast of South America find the sea unusually warm. This is because of an event called El Niño, which means "the infant" in Spanish. Usually, strong westerly winds blow the warm water to Southeast Asia. Every few years, the winds are too weak and the warm waters stay along the South American coasts. This is an El Niño season, and the warm water also heats up the air along the coast. The hot air rises, and cools to form clouds, so that rainfall is heavy and frequent along the South American coast, but sparse in Southeast Asia.

Motion in air

A ir is always moving. Air currents, or bodies of air moving in a specific direction, are constantly shifting, even in an empty room. When we walk or run, we move against the air around us. Air can slow us down. How easily an object moves through air depends on its shape.

Pushing against air

Difficult	— 5
	— 4
Moderate	— 3
	— 2
Easy	1

You will need:
- A sheet of construction paper, measuring 9.5 X 6 inches (24.1 X 15.3 cm)
- Tape
- A sheet of thin cardboard, measuring 9.5 X 6 inches (24.1 X 15.3 cm)

 1 Roll the construction paper into a cone. Tape the edge of the cone.

2 Place the cone on the palm of one hand. Hold your palm vertically, at eye-level. Run a short distance with the cone on your palm. What happens to it? Does the cone slide off your palm?

3 Repeat step 2 with the cardboard lying against your palm. Does the cardboard stay upright?

Parachutes often weigh more than 250 pounds (113 kg) and measure up to 300 square feet (27.9 m²). Why do parachutes fall slowly to the ground even though they are big and heavy?

Making a parachute!

Difficult — 5
— 4
Moderate — 3
— 2
Easy — 1

You will need:
- A silk or nylon scarf, measuring 20 X 20 inches (51 X 51 cm)
- Two pieces of string, three times as long as the scarf
- A small rock
- A piece of string long enough to go around the rock

 Tie the string to the corners of the scarf as shown.

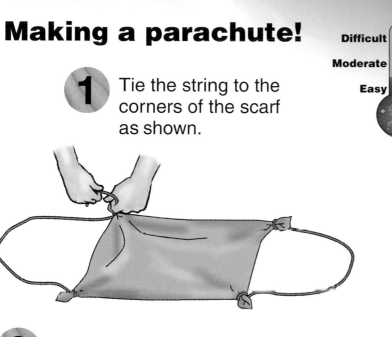

 Loop the last piece of string around the rock. Insert the other two strings in the loop so that the three strings are intertwined and hold up the rock. Knot and tighten the loop.

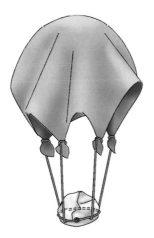

3 Wrap the rock in the scarf. Throw the rock and scarf as high as you can in the air. The rock pulls the parachute scarf open as it falls.

Air resistance

Air is made up of molecules that take up space. When we run, we move against the air that fills the space in front of us. We push against the air molecules and this slows us down. This opposing force is called **air resistance**. The amount of air resistance an object faces when it moves through air depends on the object's shape. Some shapes, such as the flat cardboard in the experiment *Pushing Against Air*, have larger surface areas, or the sizes of the surfaces of the objects. The cone in the experiment had a small surface area. An object with a larger surface area has greater air resistance acting on it, so that the flat cardboard stayed upright on your palm, but the cone did not. There were more air molecules hitting the cardboard than the cone, so the force of the molecules hitting the cardboard held it firmly on your palm. Air resistance also slows falling parachutes. In the experiment *Making a Parachute*, the scarf had a large surface area. The air resistance acting on the parachute scarf slowed the movement of the parachute, allowing it to float slowly to the ground.

I want to go faster!

Air resistance slows down moving vehicles. Scientists experiment and study the **aerodynamics** of various shapes. They have discovered that some shapes reduce air resistance, allowing vehicles to travel at higher speeds. Objects that travel easily through the air are designed to push air out of the way. The more **streamlined** an object's shape, the less air resistance it has. Less resistance lets the object move more easily through the air. Streamlined shapes are usually curved, with rounded edges, so that air flows smoothly over the surface. Airplanes and racing cars are streamlined.

Racing athletes, such as cyclists and downhill skiers, reduce air resistance by wearing helmets shaped to allow smoother airflow over their heads. Athletes also reduce the surface area of their bodies, and air resistance, by crouching.

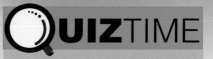

QUIZTIME

Lydia tells Paul that objects of equal weight fall at the same speed. Paul decides to test this by dropping a basketball, a pillow, an unfolded bedsheet, and a book. Which do you think falls to the floor first?

Answer: The ball, because it has the least, or smallest, surface area. The bedsheet will take the longest as it has the largest surface area.

Did you know?

Some animals are more aerodynamic than others because of their shape. The shapes of some animals let them move using the least possible amount of energy. Flying squirrels for example, do not actually fly, but glide on air using flaps of skin that act like a parachute. These animals leap off high places with their arms and legs outstretched. The flaps open and catch air, allowing the squirrels to glide.

SLOW ME DOWN!

Air resistance can be useful, especially when you do not want to move too fast! Some parachute jumpers wear suits that have flaps along the sides. This allows the jumper to increase their surface area and air resistance. The increased air resistance lets the parachute jumper fall more slowly before opening their parachutes. That way, they can enjoy the view below them for a longer time.

Wind is moving air

Wind is the energy of moving air, which produces a force. You can make wind work for you!

Floating on air

Difficult — 5
— 4
Moderate — 3
— 2
Easy — 1

You will need:
- Plasticine
- A thread spool
- Four thumbtacks
- A ping-pong ball
- A bendy straw that fits into the hole of the spool

1 Press the Plasticine over one end of the spool, leaving an opening for the hole.

2 Push the thumbtacks into the Plasticine, and balance the ping-pong ball on the tacks.

3 Put the straw through the hole at the other end of the spool. Now, blow through the straw. What happens to the ball?

When warm air rises, cold air moves in to take its place. This movement of air creates wind. This type of air movement is also used to bring fresh air and oxygen to miners in underground mines.

What goes down must come up

 Cut the flaps from the box so that one side of the box is open. Cut two holes in the top of the box to fit the two tubes.

■ Ask an adult for help

Difficult — 5
— 4
Moderate — 3
— 2
Easy — 1

You will need:
- Scissors
- A cardboard box at least 15.8 inches (40 cm) tall
- The cardboard tubes of two empty paper towel rolls
- Plastic wrap
- A candle and candle holder
- A lighter or matches

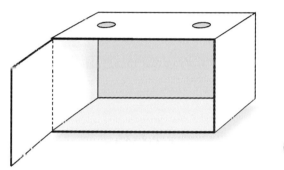

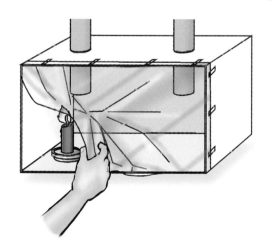

2 Cover the open side of the box with the wrap, leaving one small corner unsealed. Ask an adult to light the candle and push it through the opening in the wrap. Stretch the wrap to the side of the box so that the open side of the box is sealed completely.

 Ask an adult to light a match and hold it over the tube that is farther away from the candle. Blow out the flame. What happens to the smoke from the blown-out match?

21

Force of moving air

Moving air is a source of power. In the experiment *Floating on Air*, the ping-pong ball hovered in midair when you blew through the straw, and the moving air held the ball up. Warm air is lighter than cold air, so warm air rises and cold air sinks. Air is warmed at Earth's surface. Then it rises into the sky, is cooled, and sinks back to Earth's surface. This movement of air is called **convection**. Wind is formed by convection currents. In the experiment *What Goes Down Must Come Up*, warm air from the candle rose through the tube, and cold air flowed down the second tube to take its place. The smoke from the match was also sucked into the second tube with the cold air. Did you see the smoke from the match moving into the tube before leaving the box? Old mines were ventilated in a similar way. Ventilation systems in old mines were vertical tunnels that extended from outside the mine into the mine to circulate fresh air and push out harmful or stale air. There were often two vertical tunnels in different parts of the mines. A fire in a furnace underneath one of the tunnels heated the air. The warm air rose and moved up the tunnel. Cool, fresh air from above ground moved down the other tunnel into the mine.

The craft of hovering

A hovercraft is a vehicle that rides on air. Air is pushed against the ground, creating a force that lifts the hovercraft. A fan on the hovercraft gathers air and then redirects the air to the bottom of the hovercraft, trapping the air below. This creates a cushion of air underneath the hovercraft for it to float on. This is similar to what happened in the experiment *Floating on Air*, when you lifted the ping-pong ball by blowing air under it.

QUIZTIME

Which form of moving air has more force?
a) a hurricane wind
b) a sea breeze

Answer: a. The hurricane wind has more force. Hurricane winds have speeds up to 75 miles per hour (120.7 km per hour). The faster the moving air, the more force it has. Sea breezes have lower speeds and therefore are less forceful.

Did you know?

The hovercraft was invented by a British engineer, Sir Christopher Cockerell (1910–1999). In 1956, Cockerell tested his ideas on a model of the hovercraft made from an empty cat food tin, placed inside a coffee tin attached to an air blower, and a pair of kitchen scales!

As the wind blows, the blades of a windmill (*left*) turn a bar in the windmill. By attaching this bar to objects, people use the force of moving wind to help them do work, such as grind grain and draw water.

MIND THE MINE

In some work environments, air circulation, or ventilation, does not occur naturally. There is no proper air circulation in underground mines. Miners working so deep below the ground need fresh air to breathe. Ventilation systems are built so that miners can breathe underground. Without a **ventilation shaft**, there is no fresh oxygen entering the mine. Carbon dioxide fills the air instead of oxygen, and this makes the air dangerous for miners.

Air pressure is everywhere

Air has weight, so it exerts, or applies, pressure. Air pressure is the force of air on an object. The air around us exerts pressure, even though we do not feel it. We can feel a change in air pressure. This fun experiment shows how strong air pressure is. Be ready for a surprise!

Can crushing

1 Fill the mixing bowl with cold water.

You will need:
- A large mixing bowl
- Cold water
- An empty soda can
- A stove or hotplate
- Metal tongs
- Oven mitts

2 Pour just enough water into the soda can to cover the bottom of the can. Ask an adult to use tongs to hold the can over the heat until almost all the water has turned to steam.

3 Quickly plunge the can upside down into the cold water. What happens to the can?

Did you know that air pressure keeps airplanes in the air? Find out more about air pressure in the next experiment.

You will need:
- A push pin
- A small piece of thin cardboard
- A thread spool

The cardboard that will not blow away

1 Push the pin through the middle of the thin cardboard.

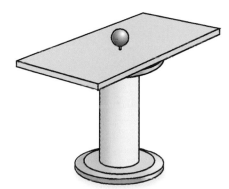

2 Place the cardboard over one end of the cotton spool, with the pin in the hole of the spool.

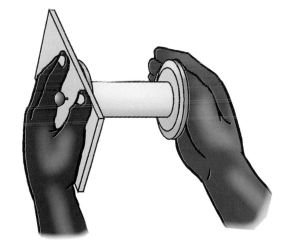

3 Blow through the hole in the open end of the spool. As you are doing so, let go of the cardboard. The cardboard stays in position, near the spool! Now, try your best to blow the cardboard away.

Air pressure exerts a force

Air all around us exerts a force on every object. Our bodies are not crushed because we have air and gases inside us that balance the outside pressure. We usually see the effects of air pressure when there is a difference between the pressure of an object and the surrounding air pressure. In the experiment *Can Crushing*, the escaping steam forced most of the air out of the can. There were fewer molecules in the can than in the surrounding air. The can kept its shape because the steam exerted the same amount of pressure as the air surrounding the can. The steam **condensed** and became water when the can was dipped in cold water. The condensation resulted in less molecules of water in the can, and lower pressure, than in the bowl. The higher pressure outside the can produced a pressure difference. The difference in pressure created the force that crushed the can.

You also saw the effect of pressure differences in the experiment *The Cardboard that Will Not Blow Away*. As you blew through the spool, you were pushing air between the spool and the cardboard. The air pressure beneath the spool became lower than the pressure on the back of the cardboard. The greater pressure pushed against the back of the cardboard, keeping it near the spool, while the pin prevented the cardboard from sliding away. The faster you moved the air, the greater the difference in the air pressure on both sides of the cardboard. You were actually keeping the cardboard in place the harder you tried to blow it away!

An ocean of air

Evangelista Torricelli (1608–1647) was the first person to understand air pressure. In 1643, the Italian physicist argued that we experienced air pressure the same way divers experienced the weight of water on their bodies. About a decade later, a Swiss mathematician named Daniel Bernoulli (1700–1782; *above*) discovered that differences in air pressure lifted objects and could help them float. This discovery was named the **Bernoulli Effect**, after the mathematician. You saw the Bernoulli Effect in action in the experiment *The Cardboard that Will Not Blow Away*. The Bernoulli Effect is what keeps airplanes in the air. Air moving over the wings of the airplane has lower pressure than the air under the wings. The differences in air pressure create a force which keeps the plane in flight.

QUIZTIME

In the experiment *The Cardboard that Will Not Blow Away,* why did the cardboard fall when you stopped blowing through the spool?

Answer: When you stopped blowing through the spool, the air pressure on both sides of the cardboard became equal. A difference in pressure was needed to produce a force that would keep the cardboard upright.

Did you know?

Air can also be compressed, or squeezed. When you pump air into a tire using a bicycle pump, you are squeezing air into the tire. Underwater scuba divers breathe air that has been compressed into small tanks. When air is compressed, its pressure increases. Compressed air is like a tightly wound spring. When the spring is released, the compressed air expands and exerts a powerful force. Compressed air is used in tools such as pneumatic drills as well as air guns.

FROM HOT TO COLD

The temperature, or hotness or coldness, of air affects air pressure. Cold air is denser than hot air, so it also weighs more than hot air. Cold air exerts more weight, and therefore more pressure, on Earth's surface than hot air. Differences in air pressure influence our weather. Air moves from an area of high pressure to one of low pressure, creating wind. The greater the pressure difference, the faster the rush of air, and the stronger the wind.

Flight

Almost all flying objects and animals, such as airplanes, rockets, insects, and birds, have wings. How do wings allow for flight?

Liftoff!

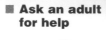
You will need:
- Two sheets of paper, measuring 8.5 X 11 inches (21.6 X 27.9 cm)
- The cardboard tube from an empty foil roll
- Tape

1 Wrap one sheet of paper around the cardboard tube to make a paper tube. Secure the edge of the paper tube with tape. Make sure that the paper tube can easily slide off the cardboard tube.

2 Remove the paper tube. Flatten one end of the paper tube and seal it with tape as shown in the diagram.

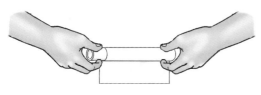

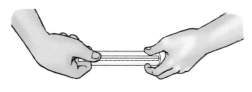

3 Make a paper shuttle by folding the other sheet of paper as shown in the diagram. Tape it to the paper tube, with the nose of the shuttle on the flattened end of the paper tube.

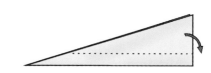

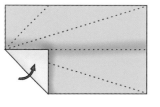

4 Insert the cardboard tube into the paper tube and blow hard through the open end to launch the shuttle!

Why do kites fly even though they do not have wings?

Make a kite

You will need:
- Scissors
- A piece of lightweight cloth, measuring 4 X 2 feet (1.3 X 0.7 m)
- A stapler
- Two thin, light sticks, one 3 feet 8 inches (1.1 m) long, and the other 20 inches (50.8 cm) long
- Strong, thick string
- Ribbons of different colors

1 Cut the kite shape as shown in the diagram, 3 feet 8 inches (1.1 m) long by 20 inches (50.8 cm) wide, from the lightweight cloth.

2 Cut four small triangles of cloth to fit the corners of the kite. Staple the corner pieces to the kite as shown in the diagram.

3 Place the sticks on the kite, and bend the sticks to fit the ends in the corner pieces.

4 Cut a piece of string 3 feet (1 m) long. Tie the ends of the string to the ends of the longer stick, and knot the center. Tie a long piece of string to the knot.

5 Tie a tail of ribbons to the base of the kite. This improves the kite's balance!

Flight

An airplane has specially designed wings to help lift it in the air. The top surfaces of airplane wings are curved. The air moving over the top of the wings travels farther than the air beneath the wings, because the distance over a curved surface is greater. This forces the air to move faster above the wings than the air under the wings. Air moving above the wings has a lower pressure than the air under the wings. It is this pressure difference, or Bernoulli Effect, that helps the airplane take off. The Bernoulli Effect also made the shuttle glide in the *Liftoff* experiment.

When we pull the string on a kite, the kite is dragged through the air, causing air to move across the surface of the kite. This reduces the air pressure on the kite's surface and makes it lighter than the air underneath. The higher air pressure beneath the kite pushes it higher, and the kite soars.

The multi-purpose kite

The Chinese invented the first kite around 1000 B.C. Some of their kites were so big and strong they could carry a person! The Chinese used these big kites to look out for enemy soldiers during wars. The kites could carry a spy and bring him over ground that was too rough for horses and carts to cross.

Throughout history, people all over the world have put kites to many good uses. Before the 1900s, photographers attached their cameras to kites to take pictures from many feet above the ground. During the American Civil War, kites delivered mail through areas where battles were fought.

QUIZTIME

What will happen if you hold a sheet of writing paper in front of your mouth and blow along the upper side?

Answer: The paper will rise! By blowing across the top of the paper, you create lower air pressure on the upper surface, and the higher pressure below the paper pushes it up. This is the Bernoulli Effect at work!

Did you know?

Kites played an important role in construction during the 1800s. In 1847, the United States and Canada were building a bridge across the Niagara River. American architect Charles Ellet (1810–1862) used kites to transport building materials over the Niagara River. Ellet used a kite to haul cables as long as 700 feet (213.4 m) across the river. The kite pulled a lightweight string over to the opposite shore, where members of his team stood. The workers could pull the heavier cables across the river using the kite string. Ellet's plan succeeded and the Niagara bridge was finished in 1848.

DEADLY BLOOD CLOTS

Blood flow in our bodies slows down under conditions of low pressure, such as in the cabin of an airplane. When this happens, blood clots may form. Why does this happen? Picture your blood stream as a river. The water in the river flows swiftly when the river is narrow. The same amount of water flows slowly when the river is wide. The water in a slow-flowing river collects in potholes in the riverbed whereas a swift-flowing river rushes over these potholes. These potholes of water are like the clots in your body. Blood clots can be deadly if they block the blood flowing to major organs, such as the heart, because they cut off the supply of oxygen-rich blood.

Glossary

aerodynamics (page 19): The interaction of air and solid bodies moving through it.

air resistance (page 18): The opposing force air exerts on objects.

bacteria (page 7): Single-cell organisms invisible to the human eye but visible under the microscope.

Bernoulli Effect (page 27): The decrease in pressure as air moves faster. The Bernoulli Effect keeps airplanes in flight.

chemical reaction (page 6): A change caused by the interaction of chemicals.

condense (page 26): To change from a gas to a liquid. Condensation usually happens when hot gases cool down.

convection (page 22): The transfer of heat in a gas or liquid. Convection currents are waves that distribute heat.

dense (page 12): Having parts that are packed together closely.

fluorescent (page 7): Glowing with bright colors produced by radiation.

force (page 14): A push or a pull.

greenhouse gas (page 11): A gas that traps heat in Earth's atmosphere.

molecules (page 6): The smallest particles of matter, consisting of one or more atoms.

oxidation (page 6): To combine chemicals and oxygen. Oxidation is a chemical reaction that often produces iron oxide, or rust.

photosynthesis (page 11): A process in which plants make food using sunlight, water, carbon dioxide, and chlorophyll, a green pigment found in leaves.

pressure (page 3): Force exerted on an area.

streamlined (page 19): Having a shape that lets an object move through water or air easily.

ventilation shaft (page 23): A passage through a mine. It allows air to move in and out of the mine.

water vapor (page 7): Water in its gaseous state

Index